Explore Mesopotamia

Zelda Wagner

Lerner Publications ◆ Minneapolis

Lerner Publications Company
An imprint of Lerner Publishing Group, Inc.
241 First Avenue North
Minneapolis, MN 55401 USA

For reading levels and more information, look up this title at www.lernerbooks.com.

Main body text set in Billy Infant Regular. Typeface provided by SparkyType.

Editor: Angel Kidd **Designer:** Martha Kranes **Photo Editor:** Elena Mai

Library of Congress Cataloging-in-Publication Data

Names: Wagner, Zelda, 2000- author
Title: Explore Mesopotamia / Zelda Wagner.
Description: Minneapolis : Lerner Publications, [2026] | Series: Lightning Bolt Books. Early civilizations | Includes bibliographical references and index. | Audience: Ages 6-9 | Audience: Grades 2-3 | Summary: "Mesopotamia was the world's first civilization. It has a history spanning over six thousand years! Readers will discover some of the many peoples that inhabited the region and what their daily lives were like" — Provided by publisher.
Identifiers: LCCN 2025013210 (print) | LCCN 2025013211 (ebook) | ISBN 9798765689233 lib. bdg. | ISBN 9798348028923 pbk | ISBN 9798765696620 epub
Subjects: LCSH: Iraq—Civilization—To 634 | Kuwait—Civilization | Turkey—Civilization | Syria—Civilization
Classification: LCC DS69.5 .W34 2026 (print) | LCC DS69.5 (ebook) | DDC 935—dc23/eng/20250602

LC record available at https://lccn.loc.gov/2025013210
LC ebook record available at https://lccn.loc.gov/2025013211

Manufactured in the United States of America
1-1012500-54791-4/4/2025

Table of Contents

The First Cities 4

Everyday Life 8

Taking Control 16

A Look at Ziggurats 20

Mesopotamia Facts 21

Glossary 22

Learn More 23

Index 24

The First Cities

Mesopotamia may have been the world's first civilization. A civilization is a group of people who live in an area together and share a culture.

Mesopotamia existed in Asia at least ten thousand years ago. It stretched from the Tigris River to the Euphrates River.

Ancient humans were mostly hunters and gatherers. But people in this area discovered they could grow food in the soil. They learned how to farm.

This sculpture from Mesopotamia shows people farming and fishing.

The soil near the rivers was great for farming.

By farming, people could stay in one place. This let them create cities, written languages, markets, and more.

Everyday Life

The first people to stay in Mesopotamia were the Sumerians. Over thousands of years, many different empires ruled the land.

Kings and priests ruled the empires. People believed their priests could talk to gods. Many people lived in cities within the empires.

Some of the earliest laws are written on this sculpture.

Builders made most buildings with mud bricks. These bricks were not very strong. This meant even important buildings such as palaces and temples were not very big.

Some people crafted tools out of different metals. They made shovels, weapons, cooking tools, and more. Other people were farmers who grew crops and raised animals.

People used gold to make jewelry.

Art was an important part of life. Artists created sculptures, pottery, glass vases, and jewelry. They also made music with instruments such as drums and harps.

This ancient instrument is called a lyre.

People spoke many languages in Mesopotamia and other nearby cultures. They often learned how to speak more than one language.

Scribes wrote on clay tablets. They used a tool called a stylus to carve the clay. Then they baked the tablets in an oven to harden them.

Many of these clay tablets still exist.

Written language began as pictures that represented words. Writing was used to keep records, communicate, create laws, and more. These writings teach us about what life was like back then.

Taking Control

After the Sumerians, many different peoples lived in Mesopotamia. They included the Amorites, Assyrians, and Babylonians.

Rome took control of the area about two thousand years ago. They ruled for about six hundred years until Arab armies took over.

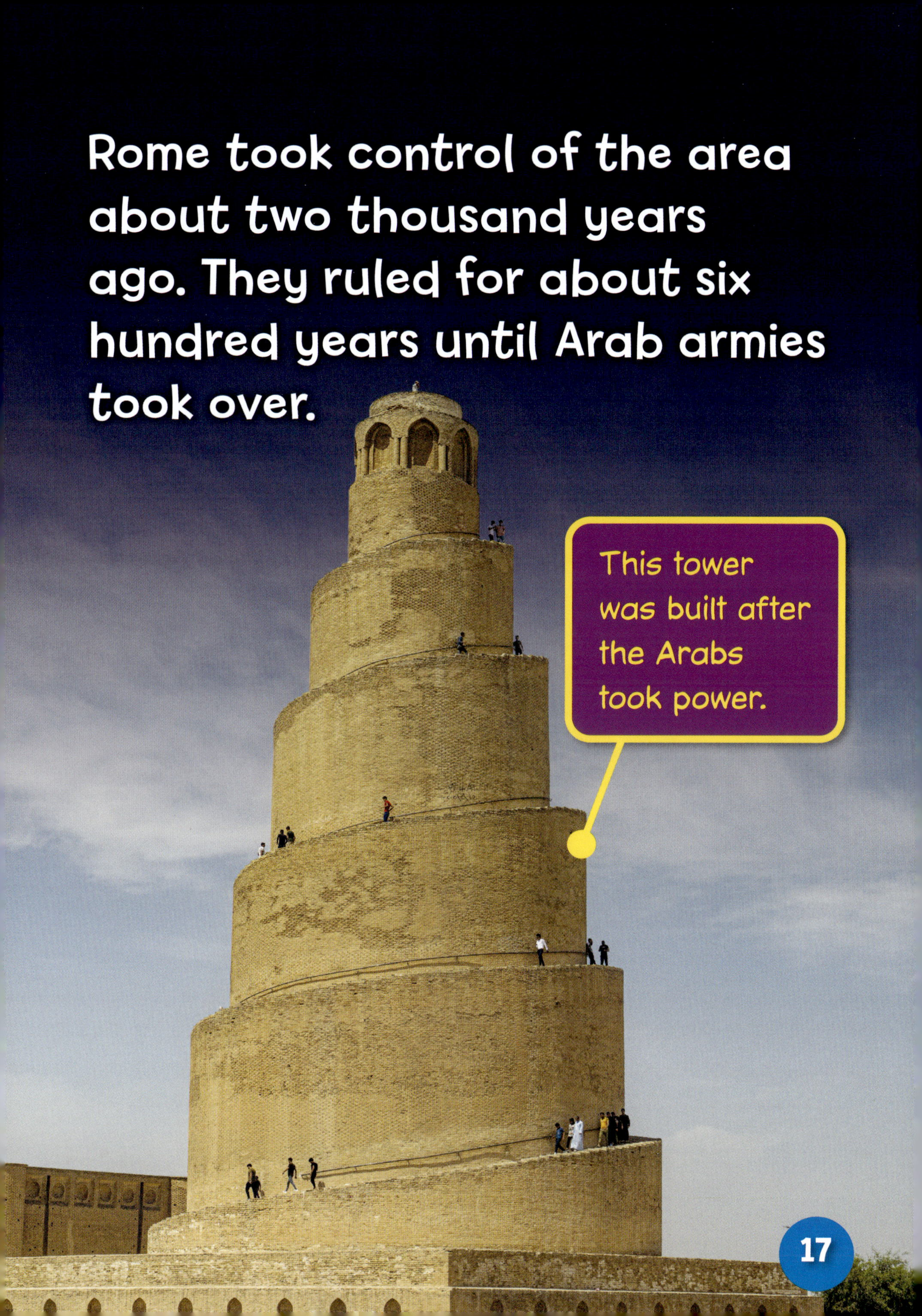

This tower was built after the Arabs took power.

A painting of an Ottoman ceremony from the 1500s

The Ottoman Empire ruled the area from the 1500s to 1918. After World War I (1914–1918), the land became part of Iraq.

There are still some ruins from Mesopotamia in Iraq. They are reminders of the beginning of human civilization.

A Look at Ziggurats

Each city in Mesopotamia had a huge building called a ziggurat. This building was made up of many stacked platforms of mud bricks. The platforms got smaller and smaller toward the top. At the top was a temple. Temples were designed to be homes for gods. Early peoples worshipped many gods. They believed gods controlled the weather, the growth of crops, and more.

Mesopotamia Facts

- People wore jewelry because they thought gemstones kept sickness and bad spirits away.
- Board games from four thousand years ago have been found in this area.
- The *Epic of Gilgamesh* is the most famous story from this time. It tells the tale of a great king who was part human, part god.

Glossary

ancient: very old

civilization: a large group of people who live in an area and share a common government and culture

culture: the beliefs, practices, and acts of everyday life shared by people in a particular place or time

empire: a group of nations or peoples under one ruler or government

hunter and gatherer: a person who survives on animals they hunt and plants they find

represent: to stand for or be a sign of

scribe: a person in ancient times who was specially trained to read and write

Learn More

Ancient Mesopotamia for Kids
http://mesopotamia.mrdonn.org

Britannica Kids: Mesopotamia
https://kids.britannica.com/kids/article/Mesopotamia/353456

Kiddle: Mesopotamia Facts for Kids
https://kids.kiddle.co/Mesopotamia

Lynch, Seth. *Ancient Mesopotamia*. Enslow, 2025.

Sabelko, Rebecca. *Iraq*. Bellwether, 2023.

Wagner, Zelda. *Explore Ancient Rome*. Lerner Publications, 2026.

Index

art, 12

Babylonians, 16

city, 7, 9

empire, 8-9, 18

farm, 6-7, 11

Iraq, 18-19

language, 7, 13, 15

priest, 9

Sumerians, 8, 16

Photo Acknowledgments

Image credits: mikroman6/Getty Images, p. 4; Laura Westlund/Independent Picture Service, p. 5; World History Archive/Alamy, p. 6; Old Books Images/Alamy, p. 7; Peter Barritt/Alamy, p. 8; Art Images/Getty Images, p. 9; Philipp Berezhnoy/Getty Images, p. 10; Metropolitan Museum of Art, pp. 11, 14; Album/Alamy, p. 12; Alireza Firouzi/Getty Images, p. 13; Bettmann/Getty Images, p. 15; Photo Researchers/Science History Images/Alamy, p. 16; imageBROKER/Michael Runkel/Getty Images, p. 17; Mehmed Osman/Wikimedia Commons (PD), p. 18; Tor Eigeland/Alamy, p. 19; rasool ali/Getty Images, p. 20.

Cover: Metropolitan Museum of Art.